Mom Hugs for Entrepreneurs

Mom Hugs for Entrepreneurs

One Woman's Lessons and Advice for Building a Successful Small Business

Raquel Gladieux

This book is dedicated to my husband, Andy, and to my children, Connor and Carly, who helped more than anyone could ever imagine in bringing the studios to life. Your "Mom hugs" fill my heart.

And …

With profound gratitude and love to our family, friends, and team that showed up and supported us throughout our business adventure—we couldn't have done it without you.

Thank you!

"It is not the critic who counts; not the man who points out how the strong man stumbles, or where the doer of deeds could have done them better. The credit belongs to the man who is actually in the arena, whose face is marred by dust and sweat and blood; who strives valiantly; who errs, who comes short again and again, because there is no effort without error and shortcoming; but who does actually strive to do the deeds; who knows great enthusiasms, the great devotions; who spends himself in a worthy cause; who at the best knows in the end the triumph of high achievement, and who at the worst, if he fails, at least fails while daring greatly, so that his place shall never be with those cold and timid souls who neither know victory nor defeat."

—Theodore Roosevelt, excerpt from his speech entitled "Citizenship in a Republic" delivered at the Sorbonne, in Paris on April 23, 1910

CONTENTS

Introduction

In 2015, after twenty-six years of serving in the U.S. Navy, I retired having attained the rank of O-5 (Commander). I enlisted in the Navy in 1989 and served a few years as a Radioman (RM) before applying to several commissioning programs. While on assignment in Australia, I learned that I had been selected to attend the Naval Academy Preparatory School, (NAPS) in Newport, Rhode Island. I graduated from NAPS after an enjoyable year learning and exploring New England and accepted an appointment to the United States Naval Academy (USNA). I spent four challenging years by the Severn River and gleefully graduated from USNA in 1995 with a Bachelor of Science degree in Political Science. Following commissioning, I served as an intelligence officer in the fleet leading sailors and navigating operational units through national security threats. Once my husband, Andy (also a USNA graduate), and I began having children, I converted to the more family friendly community of Training and Administration of Reserves (TARs as they used to be known—today they are referred to as Full Time Support (FTS) Officers). Following many happy years supporting the Navy's Reserve program, and with our kids now in high school, we decided that we no longer wanted to move or be geographically separated, so I retired from the Navy and decided to hang up my uniform and begin writing the next chapter of life.

Once I decided to retire from the Navy and my request was approved, I accepted a new position as a government contractor. I continued broadly supporting the organization that I had been supporting in uniform (now in a business suit), which I enjoyed for a while, but increasingly I became restless. I loved the people I worked with but began to feel apathetic to the work and started wondering if sitting in a cubicle and working on PowerPoint briefs was what the rest of my professional life would look like. I had also been deeply depressed following the deaths of three loved ones in close succession and seriously contemplated whether there was more to life than what I was experiencing.

At Thanksgiving in 2016, we traveled to Ohio to visit family, and I stumbled across a small creative business that I immediately fell in love with. No sooner had I walked out of the building than I was reaching out to the corporate team to learn more about whether I could open one up in our home state of Virginia. To protect myself from any potential litigation, I'm withholding the name of the business (a franchise) and will simply refer to the business as the studio. What I will say is that this was an instructional customer-facing retail/service/entertainment business built around a brick and mortar environment. The lessons in this small primer are universal, and the name of the actual franchise is really inconsequential to the business advice and lessons learned that I share.

We began the small business franchise journey in 2016 and were completely caught off guard (as everyone was) by the COVID-19 pandemic of 2020. We survived the worst of the pandemic and late in 2021, we successfully sold the last of our three locations and shifted gears to a new small business opportunity. Today, I dabble in real estate and information technology while continuing to apply the business principles I learned in my twenty-six years serving in the Navy and throughout my time running a profitable small business. I hope that my story and "Mom hugs" may in some way prove useful to you in your own business or life adventures. Whenever my kids need a pick me up or just reinforcement that they are loved and cherished, I offer them a big "Mom hug." This book includes my best advice and lessons as if they were physical "Mom hugs" to anyone beginning the journey of launching their own small business—reinforcement that you too can do it!

Take Time to Reflect: Why Do You Want to Open a Business?

When I think back to 2016, I felt like we were in this never-ending hamster wheel or rat race, and the day-to-day work routine that I was living began to feel more and more meaningless, like Groundhog Day. In fact, during that time I recall being in a budget meeting in Arlington, VA, reviewing documents and feeling like we had just had the exact same conversation, with the exact same slides, with the same people, and sharing the same questions and comments that we had the year before and the year before that, and so on. Part of the reason why we looked to open our own business was because I was losing interest in my bureaucratic government job and not being challenged enough mentally. I wanted to find work that was productive, lucrative, and meaningful.

Early in 2017, my dear friend Cindy died from colon cancer. I was devastated because she was my mentor, my godmother, and my aunt. Cindy was the person responsible for steering me toward the Navy and guiding me throughout my career. Her death impacted me on every level and made me feel extraordinarily sad and lonely. This same time period was when the young son of my boss (a dear friend, as well) committed suicide—we were all shocked, heartbroken, and devastated. After his death, we felt helpless and incapable of consoling her and her family or ourselves for that matter. A few months later; a friend's husband died tragically from sepsis, leaving behind a grieving wife and three small children (the youngest not even a year old). These losses were simply overwhelming. I felt like I was being swallowed up by grief. I realized how fragile life is and that none of us are guaranteed tomorrow. I looked at my own life and tried to reflect on whether or not I was doing what I wanted to be doing. Was I leading the kind of life that I wanted? Did I have the kind of relationships I wanted? Was there anything else that I wanted to do, make, see, or achieve in my life?

The answer for me was, "Yes." I thought, if I only had a year left to live, what would I be doing? I started thinking more and more about starting my own business and doing work that I thought I would actually enjoy doing. This would be easy to answer if I only had myself to consider or worry about, but I also had a family to factor into the equation. We had several family discussions about it and considered how it might affect our lives (of course, we could not then appreciate the profound impact it would have on our lives). I began to seriously think about starting my own business, weighing the options, and talking to my mentors to get their advice with the backdrop of *memento mori* (the eventuality of death). I think this phenomenon is called mortality motivation—if you knew how much time you had left here on earth, how would you spend it?

In my case, I was very lucky because I was already retired from the Navy and so I had a solid pension I could rely on and decent healthcare coverage. My husband had a good steady job, and we had a nice nest egg we had built up over the years. I had an inherent safety net that minimized our personal risk substantially. I knew I was very fortunate to have more options about the future than most people have. But we were definitely concerned about how starting a business might impact our ability to continue investing in our 401K plans, our kid's 529 plan, and our future.

Taking everything into consideration at this point in our lives, we decided we were ready to seriously explore starting and running our own business, and see just where that road might lead us.

My recommendation, when considering these options, is to take time to reflect on *why* you might want to open a business. Try to think as objectively and unemotionally as possible. List your pros and cons. Reflect on your lists and really ponder what it is you are looking to get out of the business or new experience. Talk to small business owners (especially people in the same line of business or within the same franchise), ask them hard questions, and really listen to their responses. Get to the core of why you think you want to open a business and figure out all the different ways you may be able to satisfy this desire. You might find that opening a small business is just one of the many avenues available to you to scratch that itch you may be feeling. Dig into all the nitty gritty details before setting off on the small business journey. Make sure you go into the process of opening a small business for sound reasons, take the time to look inward, and consider the impacts it may have on you and your inner circle of family and friends. Really consider how it might change your day-to-day life and your finances, and determine if you are ready for that.

There are Business 101 types of classes available through most community colleges, online education sites, the Small Business Administration (SBA), and, if you're a veteran, take a look at the Fleet and Family Support Center or the Morale Welfare and Recreation (MWR) or the One Stop office. Often these organizations host classes like this and others to support transitioning military members and their families. These are all great ways to gather more information about what it will take to launch a successful business and the steps to do so. If you take some time online, you can find a plethora of websites, articles, reviews, podcasts, even YouTube videos to give you all the information you need to get started!

<u>Key Takeaways</u>

- Take time to reflect on why you want to open a business and identify exactly what you hope to get out of it—be specific.
- Talk to your close family and friends and make sure everyone understands the impact it may have on your life and on theirs.
- Honestly look at your financial situation to determine if you can withstand the toll it may take on your investment portfolio.

Are You Ready to Be a CEO?

Nobody really knows what it is like to be the Chief Executive Officer (CEO) of a business until you actually do it or live with someone else doing it. People vaguely tell you that it's a lot of responsibility and that it will take over your life, but until you are in the hot seat and fully experiencing what that's like day in and day out, you just have no solid idea.

When you own your own business, that means *you* are responsible for making every decision. You own all the risk. That means that, until you can hire support, you are the person dealing with every single issue that comes up. Retail services and the restaurant businesses can be particularly demanding because you interact face-to-face with customers every single day (as opposed to something strictly online like e-commerce). If someone calls out sick before a shift, then you have to figure out how to cover it (many times that will mean you have to cover it). If materials or supplies are short, then you have to figure out a way to resolve it. If the air conditioner drain pan overflows and floods your space, then you have to figure out a way to get it fixed. If someone files for unemployment benefits, then you have to interact with the state employment commission to figure out how to resolve the matter. You have to make sure all the bills are always paid, and that payroll is always run on time. If a customer is mad about something, you have to address the issue with them. If sales are down, you have to work out how to turn that around and drive revenue up. You have to develop a sales strategy.

Often when you are small and just starting out, you may be the person answering all the phone calls and all the emails. If you approach it seriously and are determined to succeed, then the business will take priority over everything else in your life—over your family, your weekend plans, your friends, and even over other endeavors you may be involved in. Every facet of the business will occupy your time. You will be the person managing social media and creating all the marketing. Until a business is profitable enough to be able to cover the cost of additional support, you will be the person working from sunup until sundown trying to make the business successful.

It's hard, but it's also incredibly rewarding.

To be a successful small business owner is a non-stop effort that will likely consume nearly every hour of your life—at least for a while.

Before you decide to launch a new business or buy a business, be prepared to live, breathe, dream, and think about the business twenty-four seven. It will take over every spare second you have—it can be a wonderful experience filled with amazing opportunities to meet new people and push yourself to peak performance, build your own personal brand, and control your destiny, but it can also be very overwhelming. It may also be scary, and almost always exhausting in the beginning. The irony is that oftentimes people consider opening their own small businesses to be their own boss, to control their time, and to be the master of their own destiny. But really, when you own a small business, it's *the business* and your customers that control you. You actually lose much of the ability to do whatever you want, whenever you want—now as a small business owner, your business, the team, and your customers will dictate what you must do day in and day out. Are you ready to be a CEO?

Key Takeaways

- Are you prepared for nearly every part of your life to take a back seat to owning the business? Is your family prepared?
- If you have kids, are they at an age where they can help you out or be more self-sufficient so you can focus on the business?

- Do you have other responsibilities or obligations that can be set aside to run the business?

Research the Numbers

The primary reason people usually go into business for themselves is to make money, followed closely by controlling their own destiny (being their own boss). To be successful in running a business, you have to understand the numbers. You need to be intimately involved in the day-to-day accounting and the metrics or financial indicators. You must be tracking each and every dollar spent on the business and understanding your P&L (Profit/Loss) statements and financial performance details (your balance sheets). The first place to really begin to consider this aspect of the business is when you build your initial business plan and start to develop your financial framework. A business plan is where you document your company goals, operational plan, industry details, marketing and financial objectives. Developing a detailed business plan helps in identifying key elements of how your business will run and what you want to get out of it.

Spend time researching the business and understanding what it will take for the business to be financially viable. You'll want to identify the different categories of expenditures so you can build an accurate picture of what the business will cost to run. Here are a few examples of some different categories (there are many more that are not listed that might be particular to your line of business):

- Lease (this may include trash pick-up, marketing, signage fees, and monthly service on your air conditioning system—find out before you sign a lease)
- Utilities (water, gas/electric, phone, cable)
- Labor—the actual cost of the labor plus the cost of the software subscription to record employees' time and support HR functions (including your own if you pay yourself)
- Supplies (materials that you use to sell or create a product and/or food, beverage, packaging, etc.)
- Marketing (print, digital, radio, etc.)—does the corporate team (franchise) help with this?
- Insurance (you may have to pay a share of the leased building fees plus your own insurance on your property within the business to include worker's compensation and liability, etc.)
- Subscription services (YouTube, Adobe, Google, etc.)
- Website hosting fees
- Conference fees (there may be events you'll benefit from attending)

- Travel (you may need to travel for the business to be successful)
- Entertainment (networking, interviewing, staff meetings)
- Equipment necessary to run your business (capital investments)
- Vehicle expenses
- Home office expenses
- Service fees (credit card processing fees, Point of Sale (POS) fees, bank fees)
- Office supplies
- Postage, packaging, or delivery fees
- Cleaning/housekeeping fees
- Attorney fees
- Accounting fees
- Liquor license fees
- Loans (if you take any out to start the business)
- Other investments required, if any
- Taxes (you may need to pay taxes quarterly and you may have to pay city or county personal property taxes annually in addition to state and federal—find out how businesses are taxed in your local area)

Once you really dig into what the month-to-month expenses will potentially look like, then you may start to realize that the business model you had planned might not actually work. You may realize that, to really be profitable, you have to minimize your overhead (the expenses the business incurs to stay in business, regardless of its success level) or that you don't want to take on the responsibility and burden of a brick and mortar location (maybe you want to be strictly online). You may decide to open the business from home or to be in business by yourself with no employees (independent contractor for instance). Be aware that, whatever you think your monthly expenses are going to be, they are usually 10 to 20 percent higher. There will always be something you forgot to account for. There will be unexpected investments you will have to make. Factor in the cyclical nature of business. Will your business be consistent all year long? Does your business follow a normal retail cycle where the majority of the sales take place in October, November, and December (during the holidays)? If so, how will you survive during the slow summer months? Will your business be based on commission (sales for instance)?

This is where it may pay to hire someone to help you with accounting if you do not know how to do this important task alone. Hire a good small business accountant or ideally someone who understands accounting *and* taxes. Take a class with the SBA or with your local university or community college, or get on YouTube and watch some videos to learn more about how to successfully keep track of your business financial metrics and plan for taxes. Many people only look at "the numbers" at the end of the year when they are preparing their taxes, but that's too late to influence change. In order to maximize your earnings, you need to know monthly (at a minimum) what your metrics look like and how you can influence change. You should also consider creating a business tax strategy. Where can you cut costs to increase revenue? Where and how can you increase sales? Building your business plan from the very beginning (taking all of these things into consideration) is critical. Determine what it will take for the business to be viable.

These nitty gritty details are easy to overlook when you are swept up into the exciting fun and new parts of launching a business, but at the end of the day, you will have to make money to survive and even "not for profit" businesses have expenses and have to produce positive earnings. Get intimately familiar with all the financial details and know them inside and out. That way, you will quickly notice spikes or anomalies.

Here are some other questions you should ask yourself *before* starting out in a business:

- How long do you think it will take to earn back your capital investment to start the business (perform a break-even analysis)?
- What equipment will you need to invest in to start the business? Can you buy it used or refurbished?
- Will you want to start this business alone or with a business partner? How will expenses be shared?
- How much will it cost you to operate your business per customer (cost of goods sold)?

- What will the required return and the new customer rate need to be in order to grow the business?
- What are your expected daily, weekly, and monthly sales projections, and how are they determined?
- What will it take to increase sales? What if it doesn't work?
- Does the franchise or business allow you to expand your line of goods sold?
- How much will labor cost on average in your specific geographic area?
- What are your county, city, and state taxes for sales and for having employees?
- Is this business model likely to succeed? Will it be profitable enough? What dollar amount makes it worth it ($50,000 a year? $300,000 a year? $5,000,000 a year or more)?

Given the amount of *your* time that will be necessary to run the business, is it worth it to you? This goes back to your "why." What will you get out of starting a business—research the numbers and the details!

Key Takeaways

- Can you afford to lose your entire investment in the business if it doesn't work out?

- Do you understand the business model and what it will take to be profitable?
- Will I pay myself (when and how often) and what will my time be worth?

Understand the Business Details

When you are looking at business opportunities, whether you are considering opening your own business, buying into a franchise, or launching an e-commerce site, make sure you really investigate all the business details. One of the areas that I struggled with in our business was the limitations on what we were able to offer our customers. The product line and marketing material were managed by a corporate team nationally, and although there was an avenue to make suggested changes or recommendations, it was very difficult to get new ideas approved.

We lived in a very diverse area of the country with people from all backgrounds, religions, races, and languages. A number of customers and people on our staff asked me to increase our product line to include more Kwanzaa and Diwali offerings. When I pitched these ideas repeatedly to the corporate team, they fell on deaf ears. This was beyond frustrating to me. I knew in my heart that we needed to be more diverse and expand our products to be more inclusive for all of our customers, so I felt like I was disappointing everyone when I couldn't deliver on these simple requests for equitable representation.

If you seek to run a national chain franchise, be aware that you will *not* likely be making any of the decisions about the products that you will sell. Go into the business opportunity really understanding all the details of the products you will be offering your customers and the nuances of the franchise and all the legal details. Read the Franchise Disclosure Document (FDD), ask questions, or hire an attorney to help you understand it. I would caution you to make sure that, if you do hire an attorney, make sure it is someone that actually provides you value and doesn't just charge you to read documents without providing you any interpretation or valuable legal insights. Set your expectation for the service (counsel) that they are providing you *before* you sign any legal agreements for support. Ask for references to show you that they have experience in your particular business area or with the small business startup process itself. This is another area where you can get some assistance from the SBA or other niche communities focusing on helping entrepreneurs.

Before you enter any business, choose wisely and get familiar with all the business sector details, ask questions, do your own research, and get smart on the market. If you can interview other business leaders from the same company, make a concerted effort to do that—more than one or two if possible. Before we decided to open our studio, we visited several other studios and talked to no less than five other studio owners to make sure we knew what we were getting ourselves into—and we still experienced many surprises along the way! Become informed and be as unemotional about the business decision as you possibly can be. As challenging as it may be, try to think of it strictly as a business transaction.

Key Takeaways

- Representation matters, make the effort to be inclusive for all your customers.
- Read then re-read the FDD, ask questions, get help if you don't understand something.
- Do your research, make sure you understand the industry.

What Business Structure Makes Sense for You?

While you are researching all the details about the prospective new business, take some time to think about how you would legally structure the business. This aspect is very important since it affects how you will file your taxes and handle your personal liability, should something go awry. You will need to determine if you want to be a sole proprietor or want to create a partnership, a corporation, or, potentially, a Limited Liability Corporation (LLC). Determining this, and following up on state and federal licensing and registration requirements, might help you with shaping and informing your decision process. Ultimately, it will be up to you to determine which structure works best for you to satisfy your current and future needs. Do some research to really understand the details of each one. You may even consider talking to someone at the SBA or a Certified Public Accountant (CPA) who helps you with your taxes, or determine if you need to seek legal guidance.

Once you decide on the legal business structure you would like to establish, you may next have to decide on a name to give to the legal entity. Look at your options with your state's corporation commission (usually they have a website) to make sure the name is available, then you'll have to register and usually pay a small fee to legally establish the entity. If you are buying into a franchise, check with them on any naming restrictions they might have. They may not allow you to use the franchise name or anything that sounds like it, so make sure you ask them *before* you set it up. You will want to think about creating an operating agreement and articles of incorporation depending on the structure you choose (some states require this when you create a corporation). You'll be asked for proof of your legal entity (to set up a bank account, to sign a lease, etc.), so be sure to keep digital copies of all your filing paperwork.

Next, you will need to secure a business license before you can legally operate, so you'll need to register with federal, state, and local governments (all of them have a unique process). You'll want to take some time and carefully read all the documents you'll be signing to ensure you are organizing your business properly and know what the potential tax implications may be. You may be asked to identify what your NAICS (North American Industry Classification System) code is. This is how businesses are classified and often used for statistical purposes, and can also be used to conduct research on your industry.

You may want to make a trip to your local county clerk's office to ask about other specific requirements to operate. For instance, you may need to register your business name (legal or fictitious) and to potentially apply for a DBA (Doing Business As) certificate. Find out what your local jurisdictional requirements are, then file appropriately. Again, if you will be operating a franchise, ask the company if they have any specific guidance on name structure. Once you do this you may need to register for an Employer Identification Number (EIN) from the Internal Revenue Service (IRS). If you do not have any employees, you might not need to do this but it is another way to ensure you keep your personal and business interests separate. This process is a bit complicated so reach out to a professional for assistance to make sure you thoroughly understand what you are signing up for.

Key Takeaways

- Think through the business details before you make any formal commitments.
- Be aware that the business will likely have an impact on your personal taxes, so go into the endeavor prepared for all potentialities.
- Research the steps necessary to establish a business in your area, then follow the process and keep copies of everything.

Give 100 Percent of Yourself

Approach every day with enthusiasm…indeed, no great project was ever undertaken without enthusiasm, so when you endeavor to take on something new, do it with gusto and endeavor to be "all in." When we decided to take the leap and make an investment into the franchise to open our own studio, I was a little nervous about what people would say or think about our idea. Until it was open, I felt apprehensive explaining our business model to others, and I was a little bit defensive, feeling like I had to justify why we were doing it and embarrassed to be trying to do something I had no experience in. It seemed unprofessional, frivolous, and so far away from any of the government work that I had been doing my entire adult life. I felt the imposter syndrome—what background or right did I have to start a new business? What if someone found out that I didn't have any background in this new business or in running any business at all?

So many people hold themselves back for fear of what their family might say or what their friends might think, or from just the uncomfortable feeling of the unknown or even from hard work. The only thing constant in life is, in fact, change. You can only grow when you accept discomfort and accept the feelings of fear and uncertainty. Beyond fear are the rewards of an enriched life, full of new experiences, new opportunities, new people to meet, and new places to explore. Embrace every new opportunity with passion, energy, and a positive attitude. Will there be obstacles you will face? Yes, without a doubt. Will there be roadblocks? Yes, every day. Will it be scary some days? Yes, it will but you will be a better person by overcoming and embracing all of these experiences.

I'm not saying to blindly sail into the unknown, but once you have done your research, weighed your options, looked at the numbers, talked with your mentors, meditated, and spent time alone pondering the direction, then navigate that opportunity with enthusiasm and meet each challenge with a smile on your face. Lean in and give it 100 percent of your effort. It is only when you give something all of yourself that you can be satisfied internally with the outcome. Devote yourself to building the best business possible—don't hold anything back!

Once I committed down this franchise journey, I started to live, breathe, and sleep all things related to the studio and business. I wore our marketing shirts everywhere we went, and when someone stopped me to ask what our logo meant, I dropped what I was doing to explain it and gave them my business card. I put our logo on my car. I worked marketing on every social media app I could find and signed up to participate in breakfasts, lunches, dinners, and any other networking events so that I could spread the word and let everyone know where we were, what we were doing, and how they needed us to be a part of their lives. I was 100 percent "all in." Endeavor to set your ego aside and just go for it! Don't hold back—there are no rules you have to follow to successfully run a small business.

Key Takeaways

- You do not need permission to be committed to your business dream.
- Expect challenges every day.
- Be bold and creative while building your brand.

Real Estate

Once you have determined what business you want to open, this will likely lead you to the next step of determining whether or not you need a physical space to conduct your business. Even if you decide on an e-commerce business, you may find that you need a place to store your inventory or assemble your goods for shipment. The commercial real estate market is very different from the residential real estate market. I recommend you find a good commercial realtor/ broker to help you with your search. They will have access to "LoopNet" and other websites or systems to search for the perfect location. Take some time to really look around the area and get familiar with the price per square foot in different parts of town. You may find that in warehouse or industrial areas you can get more bang for your buck.

Keep in mind that not every business needs to be positioned in a main thoroughfare. If your business does not rely on foot traffic or visibility from a street, then you might be okay to rent something off the beaten path or in a less popular area of town. Be mindful of your customers though—if you expect your customers to be mostly women and will be frequenting your business at night, you'll want to pick something well-lit with ample parking and safe for them to walk alone in the dark. Make sure parking will not be a barrier for your customers. You might also consider this when negotiating your lease—do you need a loading zone? Do you need a lift gate or elevator to bring your goods in/out of your space? Do you need double doors or is a single door sufficient? Do you need a front and a back door for your customers and employees?

Another important factor is what other businesses are around the spaces you are considering leasing. Would it help your business to be near restaurants, a convenience store, or some other retail establishment? What are complementary businesses to yours and are any nearby? If you need a quiet space where your customers can think (like a kids' math tutoring business), then you might not want to be right next door to a music store that teaches music lessons. If you are a spa that offers quiet massages, then you probably don't want to be near a restaurant that has live music or a Taekwondo studio. Do you need lots of windows so your customers can see inside or do you need a shady space without windows? Do you want a drop ceiling or do you prefer an industrial aesthetic with exposed ductwork? How easy or hard will it be to cool/heat your space? If you are in a warm climate or mostly facing direct sunlight during the day, then you might want to consider shading or tinted windows and how that may impact your space. If it is a multi-story space, will having to use stairs or an elevator impede your customers? If you are on the ground floor, consider what is above you. If it is a restaurant, will the smell of food infiltrate your space? Will the sounds people above you make be an issue? Walk around the building at different times of the day and get a good feel for what the traffic flow of the day would be like. Figure out where the trash receptacles are located and how often they are emptied. Is it unsightly? Can you see the trash bins from your potential location? Do you need to be near the trash bins?

Most landlords will have very detailed demographic reports that show you the population size within one, three, and five miles of the physical location. They know the average population by age, occupation, marital status, education, household size, etc. Ask for this information so you have a good feel for the community. Ask them the traffic statistics near the location; you should factor all of these things into your decision-making process when trying to figure out where to open up your new business. Do the demographics support your anticipated customer base?

When you finally settle on a spot, then the fun begins with negotiating the terms of the lease (or purchase if you plan to buy the property). Keep in mind that, if a huge company (with a big legal team) owns the building, then you might not have much room to change the terms in the draft lease. If it is a building owned by an individual, then perhaps they will be more flexible on the lease terms. Often you have to "sell" yourself to the prospective landlord and demonstrate how your business will be good for them. They will ask you up front for a copy of your business plan or they might have a standard form that you'll have to fill out. Usually they want copies of your personal tax returns and income statements to prove your creditworthiness. Landlords are still reeling from the financial real estate crash of 2008 and from COVID-19 in 2020 so they want to make sure that you're going to pay your rent and not walk out and file bankruptcy when the going gets tough. Usually they will require personal guarantees for a certain amount of time—could be one, three, or even five years. Try to negotiate these down as much as possible.

You will have the opportunity to "red line" or edit a draft lease, so take the time to read it line by line and understand all the nuances. This may be another time when hiring an attorney makes sense, but if you have an experienced real estate broker, he or she will hopefully be experienced enough to help you with negotiating the terms so you might not need the help of an attorney. You can negotiate the amount of "build-out/tenant improvement allowance" support you get from the landlord (they may have their own construction company to help with this). What is required for you to operate your business? Do you need one or two bathrooms? Do you need a male and female bathroom? Will they let you do any of your own build-out (flooring, paint, décor, construction)?

You can also negotiate who pays for signage and where your signs will be located. Figure out the HVAC status (maybe you'll want a new unit that includes monthly service calls to change filters). They might require you to hire a company to service the HVAC and require you to provide "proof" that you have done this. Ask if the landlord does any marketing on your behalf. If they do, find out if it's on a social media platform like Facebook/META or if it's in a local magazine. Do they host any events in the plaza and are there any restrictions on what you are allowed to do outside of your space? Can you do events on your sidewalk or in the parking lot? Do they require notice to do this? How do they monitor parking and trash pick-up? If there are problems, how are they rectified? Is there always a facilities person on-site or easily accessible? Ask if there are any planned upgrades to the space. Will they be repaving the parking lot? Will the roof be replaced? Will the external façade be replaced? Basically, you need to make the effort to get as much information as you possibly can. If you need concessions for *anything* in the space you plan to lease, make sure it is included in writing in the lease. If you plan to make noise, make sure that is condition is annotated (decibels and the times you'll be making noise). They will also ask you for your operating hours. Here is a consolidated list of things to think about:

- How often is trash picked up? What happens if it is overflowing?
- Is there recycling?

- Do you have hazardous materials? How will you dispose of them?
- Do you need specialized ventilation?
- Where are the signs in the plaza and are you going to be included on them? Who pays for that service?
- Can you have assigned parking?
- Does the parking lot have adequate lighting at night?
- Does the landlord have security patrolling the area?
- Do you need a loading dock or just access to one?
- Do you need double doors or front and back doors?
- Who will your neighbors be and will their business be symbiotic with yours?
- Is the lighting inside adequate?
- What will your max capacity be and are there adequate restrooms? If not, who will bear the cost of creating new ones? Who determines how many you need and how are those calculations performed?
- Are there water fountains and do you need them?
- Does the landlord offer any marketing support? If so, how and how often?
- Are you permitted to use the area outside your leased space for events?
- Will you need security cameras or are they already positioned in the center?

- How will monthly lease payments be managed/tracked—is there an automated portal or tracking mechanism?
- How long are the lease terms (is there annual escalation of rates) and how would renewals work?
- Is it a single, double, or triple net lease? (a net lease refers to a contractual agreement where a lessee pays a portion or all of the taxes, insurance fees, and maintenance costs for a property in addition to rent).
- Would you be permitted to sublet your lease?

Once you finalize your lease, make sure you keep copies (a copy of the wet signature version and an electronic copy), as you will need these ratified copies of your lease to prove your tenancy when you call to set up utility services. Typically, the "starting day" of the lease is the day you will be permitted to open or when you get your official "certificate of occupancy" from the city/county. The entire real estate endeavor does take time. It took us over a year to find the "right" spot for our first location. We had to go through several negotiations of the "wrong" locations to finally find the "right" one. Then the lease negotiation process took another three to four months before it was finalized, and we were ready to begin working on building out the space for business. Be patient through the process and ask lots of questions along the way.

Key Takeaways

- Get professional help finding the ideal location for your business.
- Be open-minded about the different types of facilities that may work for your business.
- Everything in a lease is negotiable; make the effort to tailor the lease to your specific needs.
- Commercial real estate negotiations/ transactions work much slower than residential real estate.

Serve Others

In business, to be successful, you must figure out who your key customers are and really focus on how to give the best value possible to them. It's true. We saw that many of our repeat customers or Very Important People (VIPs) came back week after week and brought their friends, families, and co-workers along with them. We worked on making sure these customers were treated like VIPs and we went out of our way to make them feel welcome and at home in the studio—to give them a personal touch. We acknowledged and celebrated them with lots of enthusiasm, friendliness, and that special studio family love!

If you want to grow your business, then you have to take care of your customers—know who they are and work on ways to make them feel valued and appreciated. Try to find solutions to their problems. Always go the extra mile for them and make sure their experiences in your business are the best. For instance, it was important to us to make sure every one of our customers could fully enjoy our studio experience so we made sure we had an ADA (Americans with Disabilities Act) compliant studio. If you are going to run and own a successful small business, you must embrace the concept of service to others—you must serve your customers with the best care possible. Respect all of your customers, but if you know who your VIPs are, then do go out of your way to take care of them. Make sure they are heard and appreciated. Oftentimes, it was these people that would give us the best recommendations or advice for improvements. Be open to this kind of feedback and really listen to their comments or recommendations.

Embrace the journey of serving others. Sometimes it's fun, but often it's not and it's challenging, but it's all a matter of perspective. Have patience with other people and recognize that we are all on our own journey. We all have our own baggage we carry, we all have different needs to fulfill, and the only genuine way to navigate through our interactions with others is with love and patience. Be tolerant. Travel with people through their journeys with a generous heart, with your focused attention showing others that they matter, without judgment but with great enthusiasm, and always with genuine love. Nothing in life is more important than service to others and unconditional love. To live a life filled with purpose, you must learn how to serve others and to be humble. Remember, everyone has their own silent battles they are fighting, and even the people who seem to be the most hostile or confrontational may too have something they are struggling with—usually they are the ones struggling the most.

In order to build a successful business, you must do it to serve others—your customers. Do it in order to make life better for someone, to fix a problem, to make it easier, more enjoyable, to enrich the lives of others. Deliver a unique experience to your customers that they will not forget. Whether it is creating a new dating or travel app, building the next product like SPANX, creating a new service for pet owners, opening a new restaurant—whatever it is, make sure your perspective stays centered on serving others (your customers) and you will be off in the right direction. Lastly, do not be afraid to ask them for a review or feedback on their experience with you! Take their recommendations to heart and constantly improve your service to them.

Key Takeaways

- Know what problem you are solving for your customers.
- Customer service is an ongoing process (a never-ending cycle), not a destination.
- Treat your customers like royalty.

Mental Health

Being the owner of a business is a huge responsibility, and it requires a lot of hard work and effort every single day. In order to continue to make our studios successful, there were many days when I started my workday at 4:00 or 5:00 a.m. and ended it at 11:00 p.m. or later. You reap what you sow. In business just as in life, you get out of it what you put into it. If each day you endeavor to do your best and really take on all the tasks to be the best version of you possible, you will never be disappointed. It has been hard running three studios and then also juggling a full-time job while simultaneously trying to be a good mom, wife, friend, sister, aunt, neighbor—sometimes it feels like there are just not enough hours in the day to do everything, and that's because there aren't.

Don't beat yourself up trying to be everything to everyone. Focus first on yourself and treat yourself with kindness and grace. Invest in yourself daily by eating well, exercising regularly, finding quiet time to think and meditate, then focus on your family and make sure you always stay connected to the people who mean the most to you—the people that would be by your bedside should you ever be ill. Be present with your family and spend time enjoying experiences with them. Prioritize your time and the time you spend with others. If someone does not bring you joy, happiness, business goodness, and unconditional love, then do not waste your time with them. Sometimes this might mean people in your own family.

Protect yourself from people who are genuinely not interested in your well-being. If someone is demonstrating jealousy, passive aggressive behavior, gossiping, or any other toxic negative energy, then stay away from them. Find people who will bring light into your life and promote a positive mindset. Surround yourself with people that see the glass as half-full. Life will always be hard and full of challenges, so build a life full of people that react to the experiences of life with a smile on their face and with the mental fortitude to see the best in situations and look for the opportunity for growth when all seems lost. Find the people that will encourage you with sound, thoughtful advice and who genuinely care about you (through the good times and the bad times).

Honor yourself by not tolerating anyone who does not treat you with respect, kindness, and love. Forgive the people that hurt you. Building a business or being successful is hard enough as it is … don't make it more difficult by letting negative energy into your daily life. Politely let go of the people who are volatile, self-centered, and unhealthy to your mental well-being. Surround yourself with positive energy. Talk to a mental health advisor or counselor or find a personal/professional business coach or mentor as you begin your small business journey—build a strong team around you that will help you in your journey of small business success. Write in a journal and begin a gratitude practice where you consciously give thanks for all the blessings in your life and reflect on all the things that are going right. Invest in your mental well-being every single day, even if only for a few minutes.

Key Takeaways

- Your time is valuable but so is your mental health—manage it as closely as you do your calendar.
- It's okay to protect your peace—be aware of the negative energy in your life and keep it in check.
- Look for opportunities to stay upbeat and positive.

Take Care of Your Body

Your body is your temple; it is the most important machine you will ever operate. You alone control how to get your body into peak performance (and how to keep it there). You know what your body feels like when you are sleep deprived and physically exhausted. You know how this impacts your ability to focus, think, react, and make decisions. Eating, sleeping, drinking water, and exercising well are four of the most important things you can do for yourself.

When I reflect back on our time running the studio, I think taking care of my body is one of the areas where I failed. Instead of putting my phone down and taking a break from building a marketing advertisement on Facebook, I should have gone for a walk or a run. Instead of reaching for a Red Bull most afternoons, I should have taken a nap. More often than not, I would stop by Dickey's BBQ for a sandwich rather than Cava to order a salad. I didn't set a good example for how to take care of my body.

I was very lucky. I didn't experience anything more devastating than insomnia, anxiety, and depression, but those feelings all became a real day-to-day part of my life that I struggled with, and I think a large reason why I did is because I didn't put my health as my number one priority above running the business. I would have probably been a better business leader had I been more vibrant, energized, and focused as a result of better health. Life is a balance so make the effort daily to find middle ground in all the gives and takes that pull you in one direction or the other.

My recommendation to you is to make a routine out of what it takes to run your body most efficiently. *Make yourself the priority.* If running a couple of miles helps you clear the noise out of your mind, then make sure you do that every day. If staying away from red meat makes your body and digestive system feel better, then absolutely avoid red meat. Get up early and set a positive intention for the day ahead. Add walking the dog or meditation to your daily routine. Find a way to bring yourself to a peaceful and tranquil mental state besides using impairing substances. Exercise self-control and temperance in your life every day, and you will never be disappointed in the results.

You're about to embark on a new adventure that will be very challenging, and you will find it difficult to do these things every day, so instead of beating yourself up about not being able to do them all, give yourself the grace to do some of it every day. Do what you can, even if it is a small choice every day—a 1 percent difference in your daily choices can have a long-term lasting impact on your life and on your health. If you opted for a "Beyond Burger" once a month for a year (over a beef cheeseburger), that would save your body over 5,000-plus calories a year and almost an extra pound of added weight, not to mention the added stress on your heart and arteries. Take care of your body and your body will work hard for you.

Key Takeaways

- Your health is your number one resource; make smart health choices every day.
- Don't underestimate the value of a good night's sleep.
- When you fall off the wagon, don't beat yourself up. Just get back on it tomorrow.

Managing a Team

One of the most important parts of running a successful business is building a strong team. A team is a living and breathing dynamic entity that changes with each new person added or removed. When we began trying to build our team in the studio, we were looking for people who were friendly, creative, pleasant to be with, and who were eager to learn. Sometimes we hit home runs with the people we brought on the team, and sometimes we didn't. I'll be the first to admit that when I got desperate for help, I reduced my standards just to get a warm body that could help ease the burden on the schedule. But, inevitably, this would backfire. They wouldn't stay very long, or they wouldn't be a good fit, or they wouldn't deliver on the job expectations.

Retail and the services industry are hard because usually a business cannot afford to offer truly competitive wages or benefits (usually they are barely making a profit), and you have to really look for opportunities to offer "other" kinds of job perks that might keep a staff member interested in continuing to work for you. In our situation, we tried to focus on hiring people who loved the studio (past customers and friends/family). We looked for people who loved our line of business, were passionate, and also had great personalities. We took time during the interview process to really explain all the ins and outs of the studio and to go over, in detail, what the expectations were so nobody was surprised during their first shift working. We shared documentation that included all the details of what job performance would entail, and we also did a "test shift," where we explained to new hires that we were interviewing them as much as we hoped they were interviewing us to see if it was a good fit. We set up a formal training plan where a new person would "shadow" an experienced person and learn the ropes on the job in conjunction with one-on-one training with our assistant manager. We emphasized the importance of customer service and constantly reiterated that the most critical part of the studio was creating the best experience possible for all who walked through our doors.

Sometimes this onboarding training was adequate but oftentimes it wasn't. Take the time to get to know your team, to train them, to formalize policies to assist them, and to coach your team. The team members will often flourish on their own and be great contributors to the team. Be involved, come in, genuinely try to get to know them, and understand what motivates them and how to help them with their own life journey. Invest time in helping the team get to know each other as well—it will usually make coming to work more fun for everyone.

As I tried to step away from the studio and spend more time on growing the business rather than working within the business, I began to feel disconnected from the staff and also from the customers, so I would re-engage and make sure that I was continuing to plan fun staff events where we could address issues with the studio collectively as a team and also have fun while building camaraderie and *esprit de corps* among the team members. Create a fun environment where people get to know one another and have fun coming to work, and look forward to it. I genuinely cared about each person on the team (still do), and I think people knew that. But I would be lying if I said it was always rainbows and sunshine.

Remember—sometimes it is lonely at the top. That means that, when you are at the top leading or managing people, you cannot be everyone's friend. This doesn't mean that you can't be friendly to everyone, but it does mean that you need to hold people accountable for their actions and, sometimes, you have to have difficult conversations or make tough decisions. Don't bury your head in the sand and ignore a bad situation. Address it head on and try to resolve it as amicably as possible. Always praise in public and reprimand in private. When I had to correct behavior with counseling sessions, I would set up private face-to-face appointments with the individual, then I documented the conversation and had us both sign the performance review. After that,

I moved on and tried not to hold it over their head. Sometimes you will make people mad when you call out shortcomings, so be prepared for the reaction you may receive.

One time, a lead team member left the studio in less than stellar shape following an event and, when I reached out to her to find out what happened, she flipped out. She was enraged that I called into question her not following the closing checklist, that I questioned her leadership, that I did it over the phone, and that I didn't stop to ask if there was some mitigating circumstance. I think her general feeling was that I was lucky to have her and not the other way around. She quit on the spot. The lesson in this for me was not to react too quickly to a situation. Think about it for twenty-four hours (sleep on it), set up a meeting with the person to discuss it face-to-face, ask questions and then, if the person still has a belligerent attitude or refuses to adhere to your documented standards, then agree to part ways amicably.

I worked really hard to always treat other people as I would like to be treated, but often that wasn't reciprocated. When you're in charge, sometimes you won't be treated with respect or dignity; don't take it personally. Sometimes people will use you, lie to you, and treat you unfairly, but what they do and what they think are none of your business. Your business is you and how you choose to react or respond in those situations. Always take the high road—be the better person, or, as Michelle Obama says, "When they go low, we go high."

Set a standard and hold everyone accountable to that standard—don't treat people differently. I discovered one of our employees was stealing from us, and I fired her on the spot. No matter what—lying, cheating, and stealing should never be tolerated. Absolutely never ever gossip or talk about people. That is petty, unprofessional, undignified, and will only discredit you as a leader. If you don't have anything nice to say, then don't say anything at all! Earning the privilege to manage a team is a wonderful opportunity that you should never take lightly. Invest time in your people and work day-to-day to create a high-performing team that cares for and respects each team member. I enthusiastically worked alongside everyone on our team, and no job was beneath me—I cleaned the bathroom, scrubbed the floors, organized inventory, etc. I never asked someone on my team to do something that I wasn't willing to do myself, and I worked hard to set a good example of how tasks should be completed. I built an exceptionally strong team that had a clear purpose, trusted each other (and me), and knew what the studio vision included. Invest your time building a strong team and make sure they know how much you appreciate them.

Key Takeaways

- It is a privilege to manage a team—treat your people with respect, empathy, and care.
- When tough situations arise with your team, take time to reflect and let it "simmer"

if you can before you take any action. When you do act, document it.

- Avoid gossip and create an environment where people lift one another up rather than tearing each other down.

Celebrate Your Best Employees

One of the things that there never seems to be enough of but that we all have equal amounts of is time. Use your time wisely. Protect your time. In growing a business, you will always have competing demands for your time. Learn how to manage your time effectively. Avoid wasting your time on people or pastimes that don't bring you anything productive or positive in return. You've heard the 90/10 rule of spending 90 percent of your time on 10 percent of the people. You have to actively resist this day in and day out. Don't get bogged down in drama between people at work, and the number one way to avoid this is to not gossip or participate in conversations about other people as much as humanly possible. Keep your relationships with your team and your customers professional—always.

Protect your mental health and peace by steering clear of people who are dysfunctional and constantly causing chaos; people who churn wherever they go. You have a choice on who you allow into your inner circle so choose carefully. If you notice that there's someone on the team who is perpetually causing problems or always in the middle of animosity or negative situations, then you should think objectively about how to let them go. Do not tolerate poor performance. Address it directly, empathetically, and privately, then document it and file it away. Let the negative person on the team who never has anything positive to say go. Counsel the person that has a bad review from a customer once, then if there is a second time, let them go. Invest your precious time in boosting up and helping the good and productive people on your team—spend time giving them additional training, recognition, and helping them out as much as you can. Listen to their recommendations for process improvements and reward their excellent contributions as much as you possibly can. Take their feedback to heart. Celebrate and reward your best employees so you are able to retain them and continue to push them forward and help them achieve their own personal goals.

One of the ways we did this was to give Starbucks gift cards (usually five-to-ten dollars each) to each person when they were specifically called out in a social media review or if a customer pointed out one of our staff members in an email message. This was a great way to acknowledge outstanding performance and to show everyone on the team how much we cared about customer service and recognized their hard work. We also gave key employees bonuses periodically to make sure they knew how much we appreciated their role on the team. There are lots of ways to pat your best employees on the back—take the time to do this and be creative in letting them know how much you appreciate them. It will improve your retention, and it's important to acknowledge the people that have a role in making the business successful.

<u>Key Takeaways</u>

- Great employees are priceless—treat them well.
- Provide feedback in a caring, compassionate, and factual manner.
- Celebrate your employees and say, "thank you" when they go above and beyond.

Ask for Help; Blaze a Trail

I think a portion of what determines whether or not someone will be successful in business and in life is their grit and tenacity. When you have a gigantic task in front of you that's important to you, don't get overwhelmed looking at the entirety of the task, but rather put your head down and accomplish one piece of the task at a time—one bite of the elephant at a time, if you will. Visualize yourself every day achieving your goals. What will it look like when you are done? What will it feel like when you get there? How will you celebrate your accomplishment? Think to yourself, "What one step can I take today toward accomplishing my goal?"

When we set about opening the first studio location, we experienced one setback after another. There seemed to be never-ending roadblocks that, at the time, felt insurmountable. We felt like we were navigating uncharted seas figuring out the nuances of the city permitting process without really understanding the mechanics of how to get our site plans approved. I reached out to the local

SBA office to ask for help. I was paired up with an experienced business owner/advisor who gave me some solid recommendations for what to do next. He recommended that I go to the county permitting office in person and spend some time talking to each of the reviewers (fire marshal, mechanical engineering, electrical engineering, structural engineering, etc.) who had questions about our blueprints and answer their questions in an effort to get things approved. I did this for a week—meeting face-to-face with the people who had the ability to sign off on our plans. We also hired an architect to assist us in re-drawing and streamlining our plans and finally, after almost a year, we were given the green light to go ahead to begin our build-out!

What's the moral here? Ask for help. Be detailed and direct and ask for exactly what you want. Sometimes it's not enough to methodically set about completing tasks to achieve your goals or visualizing what completing your goals looks like. Sometimes (in fact, many times) you will need to ask for help. Don't ever be afraid to ask questions; be the person in the room that raises their hand if something truly does not make sense. Nine times out of ten there are usually other people in the room who don't understand or have the same questions. Be polite, and respectful, but ask the question. Listen carefully to others but, if it still doesn't make sense, find someone who can explain it to you. Take the initiative to figure stuff out and, when you get stuck, ask for help—Google it, look it up on YouTube, ask a mentor, ask a friend, ask someone who has been through this process before you, post it out on social media for a collective response (be prepared to potentially receive some negative or less than helpful responses). Don't waste time feeling sorry for yourself—do something to fix the situation when you get stuck. Of course, being a Naval Academy graduate, we frame this concept around the story: "A Message to Garcia"—figure it out like 1st Lt. Andrew S. Rowan did in Elbert Hubbard's 1899 essay. Show that you have grit in everything that you do—always give YOUR best, every single day.

Key Takeaways

- When you can't figure something out, ask for help.
- Take the initiative to fix problems.
- Be tenacious.

Be Methodical and Patient

Focus on the details. When the restaurant above our studio flooded and drenched our foyer due to an overflowing mop basin and sink that was not turned off, it caused a ton of damage and destruction to the studio. My first inclination was to quickly address the situation, and get it repaired as fast as possible so we could reopen for business. Sometimes it is best to slow down and evaluate the entirety of the situation before deciding what to do next.

In this instance, I was so anxious to hurry up and get the water turned off and the space repaired that I didn't contemplate all the options I had before deciding on a plan. I called our insurance company and began getting them involved for assistance almost immediately. I should have waited and worked with the building supervisor to see if the landlord would have brokered all the repairs on my behalf and dealt directly with the restaurant that was to blame for the entire mess and *their* insurance company instead of getting my own insurance involved.

In a crisis, you need to slow down and take an accurate snapshot of the situation. I really do mean taking photos and video to record everything that happened and document what was damaged. Take notes and keep records of who said what, and don't leave anything to chance or misinterpretation. Write the events down in a journal and cite who said what. When the flooring needed to be replaced because of the water damage, the insurance company didn't want to replace all the flooring in the entire studio. But by not doing so, it created a seam from the foyer to the work area, which was a trip hazard and also a pain when we had deliveries that needed to be wheeled over it with a pallet jack. I should have required the entire floor to be replaced in the whole studio or at least finger joined with the foyer (so there was no beveled lip). The other issue was that, I wasn't there when the flooring was done, and the contractor did a terrible job of lining the wood up, so it looked lopsided. Again, I should have had someone there to oversee and micromanage the entire project because oftentimes nobody does things the way you expect or want them to unless you are physically there to provide direction and oversight. Articulate your expectations and oversee the details—don't leave anything to chance or assumptions.

I spent a lot more of my time dealing with the insurance companies than I should have or would have, had I just waited and let the building supervisor continue to work to resolve and fix the damage with the offender's insurance company. The takeaway is to be patient and less in a hurry to check things off the list—sometimes in life it's better to be methodical, detailed, and take things slowly. Often the result is fewer headaches for yourself. Catch your breath and sleep on it before being too quick to resolve a problem.

Key Takeaways

- In an emergency, take photos if "evidence" may be needed.
- Look at the big picture before rushing to a solution.
- Personally direct completion of tasks if you expect a certain outcome.

Money

Most people that want to open a small business need to take out business loans to get started. Usually they reach out to the SBA, begin doing research, and start talking to different banks to see if they can get a good interest rate to borrow whatever resources they need to get started. These loans are usually pretty expensive and sometimes pretty tough to get with steep interest rates and short payback periods. The bank wants to see the business plan and all your personal finances to determine if they are making a sound investment in you and your new business. Landlords or leasing/commercial real estate offices do the same thing. They don't want to lease a space to someone that may be a financial liability. They run credit checks and ask for copies of personal bank statements, your professional resume, references, tax records, and lots of other documentation to "prove" that you know how to manage money and are not a financial risk. Further, they often require "personal guarantees" for three or even five years, which is a legal promise to personally assume and repay any debt the business accrues (even if the business is within an LLC or some other business legal arrangement).

Franchises also perform their due diligence to verify that you know how to manage money well, have professional experience related to running a business, and have a high probability of successfully promoting their brand. Some highly profitable and desirable franchises are really tough to break into (Chick-Fil-A for instance), and most require a pretty hefty upfront investment of $25,000 to $200,000 just to start off. In order to survive the first year of business operations, it is usually recommended a start-up have at least another $50,000 in reserve (depending on the scale of the business) until the business is able to "break even" on the initial investment and survive on its own.

In our case, we had saved money and created a little nest egg that we had decided to leverage, to start the business. We didn't have to take out any loans to get started, so we assumed all the financial risk personally. We also made a commitment to work in the studio as much as possible in the first few years to reduce labor costs and increase our profit margins. This meant that many days, I would work all day in my regular (day) job then drive to the studio and work all night resulting in many eighteen-hour days. We would take turns working evening shifts after our day jobs to make sure someone was always home with the kids. I'd be lying if I said it was easy, because it wasn't—it was really hard, but it was also fun and exhilarating. As we trained up more and more of the staff, and the revenue stream became more regular (and we paid ourselves back for our initial investment), we began to hire more staff and spend less time personally running every workshop.

During the first few years of owning the business, we did not pay ourselves at all. We didn't pull any money out of our business accounts so we would have the opportunity to expand when the time was right. We knew from the very beginning that, to maximize our earning potential, we would have to open up multiple studios. So, when we were told that there was outside interest from new people looking to open up locations near us, we decided to open up additional locations instead of having new owners competing with our geographic location. We had expressed interest in expanding with the corporate leadership, so we were given the first right of refusal. Now when I reflect back on this decision, I realize we made the decision to expand too quickly without really considering the impact it would potentially have on our lives. In hindsight, we should have been more patient and methodical in weighing all our options (as recommended in an earlier section).

We initially thought the second location we opened would be great to expand our customer demographics but was actually very hard because it was far away from home, and we didn't really know the market as well as we thought we did. We chose an area that was tough to break into, and we didn't have a local person that could help us spread the word and drive new business. Thankfully, the monthly lease we had there was pretty low so we could afford to operate it in the red (with a deficit) until the business took off (which took much longer than we ever expected). It was hard to keep good help in this location, as well, because it required so many hours operating alone and really needed a manager who was a self-starter able to hit the sidewalk to make contacts and drum up business. It also required someone who was trustworthy, wouldn't violate any of the business tenets, and would be of sound moral character. Finding good help proved to be very challenging— especially because, in retail, you're usually not able to offer competitive salaries (again, due to very thin profit margins) and, therefore, we always struggled with manpower in our second studio.

The third location we expanded to was a great physical location in a growing area with lots of potential, but it was also very expensive and far from home. This meant I was on the road a lot, driving between all three studios once they were all up and running. At this point in time I quit my "day job" and was 100 percent focused on managing the three studio locations. In order to save money, we were making a lot of the base materials ourselves (which was a very bulky, manual and time intensive process) and this became increasingly challenging. We had a seasoned manager in the third studio, so that helped, but we also noticed that the second and third locations began pulling some of our "regular" customers away from the first location. Day in and day out, I began to feel like I was stretched way too thin and the first location began to suffer from my inability to give it the attention that I needed to.

Then the Pandemic Hit in March of 2020

At first, we thought we would only have to close the studios for two weeks. Then, when we realized it would have to be for much longer than we originally anticipated, we began to get really scared. If we could not open our doors for business, how could we make enough money to cover the cost of all of our bills? We still had business savings, and we heard about this new Payroll Protection Program (PPP) that was just starting, so we hunkered down and took it one day at a time. Our expenses were pretty pared down. We never went wild spending any of our earnings from the first couple of years. We also saved and reinvested back into the businesses. Luckily, we had a buffer of savings that got us through the worst of the pandemic. We didn't overextend ourselves early on, so we didn't have to make decisions out of sheer desperation or scarcity.

The lesson I want you to learn from this is the importance of financial discipline, which will be the foundation for financial freedom. The only way you attain that is by saving your money and finding ways to make your money work for you. Live within your means and create emergency savings and your own nest egg that you can always lean on in a dire emergency or in a pandemic. Avoid the temptation to live lavishly—save your money. In business (just as in your personal life) each dollar you save is a step toward living your life on YOUR own terms; financial stability equals freedom. Be frugal with your earnings and become financially independent.

Key Takeaways

- Be modest with your resources—you never know when the next rainy day is coming.
- Understand the financial details of your business daily.
- Build reserves so you can survive for a few months if confronted with a crisis.

Lessons Learned from the Pandemic

In March of 2020, the COVID-19 Pandemic caused global chaos. People and businesses are still reeling from it today, and we will all likely still be feeling the impacts for years to come. Nobody could have predicted it or prepared for it adequately. Our business depended on customers and people interacting with our staff face-to-face, so when we had to close our doors indefinitely, the impact was profound. It was terrifying watching the news and, aside from the fear of getting sick ourselves, we were very worried what the impact would be to our businesses. We had three brick and mortar locations and a large team that we employed to support them.

We tried to quickly pivot to offering our customers a "take home" option but were quickly directed by our corporate office to cease and desist from this due to safety concerns and potential legal ramifications. Our network of other franchise owners quickly began communicating to try to brainstorm different things that we could do to continue generating revenue.

The corporate team was slow to assist the studio owners with ideas, and this lack of engagement created a lot of animosity and frustration for studio owners struggling to make ends meet.

In the early days, there was no discussion of government support, and our landlords were not equipped to begin having discussions with us about modifying the terms of our leases. We had to keep paying all of our bills despite not having any customers in the studio or solid revenue stream. Our savings account began to drain quickly, and we knew we had to do something to stop the hemorrhaging. We tried to quickly adapt to the changing situations and really scale back the staff. This was also tough because many people depended on their full-time or part-time wages, so we had to make the tough decisions to let some people go. The pandemic brought out the best and the worst in people, which I think we all saw across the entire country. Some people were flexible and helpful, and some were not. Some people on our team offered to help us out (even without pay), which we are still grateful for.

I'm not sure how to recommend preparing for something as catastrophic as a pandemic, but what I would recommend is to always be flexible in the face of adversity. Don't be tempted to waste your time complaining or whining with naysayers. Ask for help from others if you need it. The pandemic gave us a great opportunity to serve others—we had some customers and staff that asked to use the studio in isolation from others, which we did, and it afforded many people from our team the chance to get out of the house and do something fun with the people they were isolating with. I am grateful I had the chance to give back to our team and the community in this way.

When the Payroll Protection Plan (PPP) was being introduced, it created a frenzy in the banking community. Nobody seemed to know how to file the SBA paperwork correctly, and the media created a scarcity mentality—if you weren't one of the first businesses to apply for it, you might not get any help. It took a long time for the applications to become available and, when they did, it was a long process that required a lot of administrative documentation in order to be properly submitted. We reached out to the two different banks that we had been using in our personal lives for over thirty years, and neither one of them was responsive. We spent hours and hours on the phone trying to get questions answered. We shed a lot of tears out of frustration and fear. Instead of continuing to bang our heads against the wall, after a few days, we finally went to different banks and applied through different channels, and were ultimately successful with securing a small PPP loan. My advice is to adapt to overcome challenges when confronted with them. Don't be satisfied until you get the help you need, and be aware that it might come from someplace totally unexpected. Another avenue of support we received came from one of our landlords (without solicitation from us), who was willing to give us a grant to cover a few months of our lease. I think part of the reason they offered this was because we kept on paying our rent through the early months of the pandemic and because we didn't join other tenants in signing petitions or agreements aimed against the landlord. This particular landlord went out of his way twice to work with us to reduce our lease payments in order to help get us back on our feet.

We saw so many other businesses in our plaza close up as a result of the pandemic. We took a long look at all three of our studios and talked about where we saw ourselves one, three, five, ten years from now, and realized that we were ready to move on to something different. We realized that we had gotten out of the business experience everything that we wanted and that we were ready to move on to the next chapter of our lives. We continued trying to grow the business back up through the pandemic and began working on finding new owners that would love the business and studios as much as we did and continue to grow and give back to the communities we loved.

You are going to experience setbacks in your business. Unexpected bad things will happen; how you deal with them (persevere) and react to them is what will set you apart from everyone else out there. My recommendation for surviving through these tough times is to be as resilient as you possibly can be. Be creative, show some grit, and be willing to take recommendations from others on how to survive. Ask for help from others and have grace with yourself while overcoming obstacles. Remember, as

Marcus Aurelius put it sometimes, "The impediment to action advances action. What stands in the way becomes the way."

Key Takeaways

- In the face of adversity, be as creative as you can be to overcome it.
- Sometimes when you feel stuck, it helps to give back to others—volunteer to help someone else out and you might uncover some potential solutions along the way.
- Be receptive to asking and receiving help—it may come from a place you least expect it.

Moral Compass

One of the most fundamental tenets to being an exceptional leader is to have moral courage. When nobody is looking, do you do the right thing? This sounds easy enough, but it really should permeate through everything you do as a leader. If a customer overpays, do you let them know and give them back the difference? If you see someone on your team treated poorly, do you step in to correct the situation?

At your very core, you must have your own set of personal values that you stand by and never waiver from—a moral compass. When confronted with ethical or moral dilemmas, you can lean on your values to help guide you in determining the best way to respond. What are your personal core values? Are you willing to stand up for them? Do you have the courage to do the right thing in a tough situation?

In business, especially if you lead the business, you must make it known what the mission of the organization is. Make sure everyone knows what you stand for and where you are going—what your vision and guiding principles are. Publish your business mission statement or your vision so everyone knows what it is. If everyone knows this and sees YOU upholding your values in every interaction, then when you are not there, they should know how to react to any situation. They should be able to ask themselves, "What would the boss do?" then act accordingly.

Organizations embody and assume the values and ethics of their leaders. Demonstrate your values in your actions, your examples, your words, and the commitments you make. Set the moral tone from the very beginning and continuously create a culture of integrity, compassion, forgiveness, responsibility, and love. Can you look at yourself in the mirror at the end of the day and say, "I did my very best"? In all my interactions today, did I uphold my core values? You may stumble on this some days, and that's okay, but endeavor to make it right tomorrow and the day after that. Don't succumb to corporate pressure—if something doesn't feel right, then it probably isn't. Always do the right thing.

Key Takeaways

- Articulate your values to the team.
- Live your values every day.
- Reward your team for upholding your principles.

Network

It is lonely at the top. It is important to find a network of mentors to collaborate with. Find other successful CEOs or business executives to talk with, to meet with, to discuss challenges with, and look for opportunities to help each other out. Don't worry if they're not in your same business sector or if they are older or younger than you, male or female—they don't have to look at all like you, so be open minded. Search for ways to improve your thinking and sharpen your thought processes. Participate in mastermind events, seminars for business improvement, read/listen to books, listen to Ted Talks, webinars or podcasts—never stop learning and looking for opportunities to improve. Sign up for self-improvement seminars or with the local SBA or Chamber of Commerce networking events. Proactively look for ways to continue learning and to meet other people doing the same thing.

An area of the business I enjoyed building tremendously was my relationships with all our vendors. It took a lot of time and effort to personally get to know our national sales reps, the delivery people, our suppliers, our insurance team, the corporate team, other studio owners, other local small businesses, and basically anyone that I routinely interacted with in the course of running our business day-to-day. The investment of time to get to know all of these people individually was rewarding and delightful.

Knowing the suppliers personally meant that, when the pandemic hit and supplies began to become scarce, the team in some of those offices put supplies to the side for me without me having to ask. When I needed a last-minute order, the vendor shipped mine early ahead of everyone else's, and I always tried to express as much gratitude as possible. The relationships you build day in and day out of your lives are important, and they create the fabric of a good life. A community where you are surrounded by people that genuinely care for you, and you for them, is priceless—this will be an environment where it is easier to get things done because you are looking out for one another. Don't burn bridges. Look for ways to salvage friendships and repair broken relationships whenever possible.

Take the time to get to know the people in your neighborhood (as Mr. Rogers would have said). Invest time getting to know other business leaders and share in the experiences of life with them. Listen to them more than you talk. Patronize their businesses and look for opportunities to return the favors. Build a community and be a contributor to making it better. Make an active effort to network as often as you possibly can.

Key Takeaways

- Network to find other business leaders that you can share experiences with and help one another out.
- Get to know the people you interact with every day—look out for one another.
- Keep refining the craft of leadership and management within your team and your community.

Marketing to Increase Sales

For an introverted leader (like me), one of the scariest things about owning your own business is constantly putting yourself out there and making the effort every day to connect with people to promote your business. Marketing yourself and your business is essential to increasing revenue, and figuring out who exactly your customer is and how to offer something to them of value is key to your ongoing business success. You don't have to be a "spotlight ranger" that constantly looks for ways to be in front of a camera or have your face or name plastered on everything that you do, but you do have to understand your customers' wants and needs and figure out how you can provide those valuable things to them. You must be creative and also a little curious to try new methods of marketing to heighten brand awareness and drive sales up.

Look for opportunities to collaborate with people to cultivate new methods to deliver new products or services. I cold-called someone once that I found on a community Facebook page who looked like she had a new successful business that could be complementary to ours. We coordinated via email then finally had a long phone conversation before making an agreement to have a collaborative event— it was so successful that we sold out a year's worth of monthly teamed up events and they still continue this collaboration with our studios today! The hidden blessing in this is that I also made a wonderful new friend and got to co-mentor another small business owner.

Be open minded and always look for opportunities to grow your business or your office and putting yourself out there to meet others, collaborate, and network. Finding opportunities to connect and leverage your network of talented people is fundamental to business growth. Try new things, go the extra mile to meet people, connect with them and think outside the box—successful businesses figure out how to deliver value or solve a problem for their customers sometimes before the customer even realizes it. Use your Customer Relationship Management (CRM) tools (technology used for managing relationships and electronic interactions with customers) effectively. Automate electronic tools as much as possible. Create automated responses in social media platforms to commonly asked questions and leverage technology to perform a lot of the time-consuming tasks (email marketing for instance). Pay attention to what works and what does not work. Try different tactics and strategies. Figure out how to leverage Search Engine Optimization (SEO) and other digital media avenues (improving your website to increase product visibility on search engines) or find someone that can help you figure out how to do it. Use Google alerts and other useful online business tools.

Owning a small business is hard so make sure you also are supporting other small businesses. Look for opportunities to lift them up, advertise for them, and encourage other people to patronize their shops or services. Share ideas with them and make constructive recommendations to help them grow as well. Employ marketing tools at the grassroots level and with digital content and other opportunities that you see to expand business awareness.

I had a USNA classmate that worked for Google, who I saw on a social media post. He made a comment about how Google supports veterans. I reached out to him to say, "hello" and tell him how much I appreciated the "Google Veteran Small Business Owner Coin" that I had received in the mail. He was excited to hear that and asked if I would be interested in potentially being profiled in their upcoming Google Economic Impact Report. Would I? "Absolutely," I said! Many months later, this resulted in an all-day photo/video shoot and a full "success story" profiled in their global annual economic impact report—wow! Go ahead, lean into opportunities to meet and talk to people to share your business story. You never know where it may lead! Without pushing your limits, without daring greatly, you will never know what is truly possible.

<u>Key Takeaways</u>

- Be creative with how you attract new customers (marketing).
- Marketing is an on-going effort, mix up your activities and automate tools as much as possible.
- Find marketing help if/when you get stuck.

Know Your Competition

When you are starting out on your entrepreneurial journey, take the time to understand the market and your competitors. Make sure you know who they are and what they are offering so you can position yourself for the best value proposition possible for your customers. What will you be offering them? Is it the same as your competition? Is it different, how so? Will your product or service be the same price? How will you direct customers to your website instead of to your competitors? How will you be unique? Find your business niche.

This is where you must know who your customer is inside and out. Really zone into your target—not just twenty-to-twenty-five-year-olds, for instance, but twenty-to-twenty-five-year-old women, college educated, middle class, located within forty miles of a particular zip code that like to listen to country music and shop at Target. Find out what your customer sweet spot is and really target your marketing to your audience. Hopefully, your market will grow and you'll get more interest in your business as it evolves. But start off, more narrowly, on finding out who you think your ideal customer is and ask yourself, *What do they need that I'm offering? How do they consume information? Do they use social media, and if so, which platforms?*

You should know your competition well. Take the time to periodically take a look at what products or services they are offering. You may find that they are offering customers something amazing that you can copy or leverage to offer something similar. I caution you not to spend too much time focused on your competitors because you really want to be creative, original, and responsive to your customer needs (not constantly mimicking your competition). You don't want to be biased or have your thinking unduly influenced by what others are doing. Break new ground, generate new ideas, and be creative. Poll your customers and ask them what new products or services they want, seek feedback and reviews online, and listen to the responses you receive. Are the products you are offering your customers better today than what you were selling yesterday? Constantly strive to improve.

In the studio, I tried to teach the staff how to deliver the best customer experience possible. I tried not to imitate our competitors or to offer similar sales/deals that they were offering. I put a lot of energy into being original and trying to shape ads and specialized offerings that I thought the customers would enjoy, based on conversations with them and with the staff. Our team always gave outstanding feedback and generated wonderful ideas on how to improve the services and products we offered—we were so lucky that our team was fully engaged and willing to constantly make the studio better. We held monthly staff meetings where we actively sought feedback and brainstormed with our team to solve problems. We valued every member of our team and worked hard to reward them with free perks and tried to make the studio environment as fun as possible. Build a great team and you, too, will be able to encourage everyone to get invested in making your product or service the best it can possibly be. Temper your ego and be willing to accept great ideas for product or service improvement wherever they may come from!

Key Takeaways

- Know your competition and figure out what sets you apart.
- Refine and master the business areas where you are unique.
- Be receptive to feedback.

Be Authentic—Just Be Yourself!

For the longest time, I felt like I had to get permission to do anything or that I had to stay within the lines of my lane and do what was expected of me. Even when we launched the business, I was afraid to veer off course too much for fear of getting reprimanded by the corporate office or people not liking me or thinking I wasn't doing a good job. Maybe it was my military background or because I wanted everyone to like me or because I put way too much emphasis on my ego—my sense of self-esteem and importance.

When I slowly became more confident in myself as a business owner and as a CEO, I started to pay less attention to seeking the approval of the corporate team. I worried less about getting everything approved through the corporate team. I started to take more risks and be a little edgier in my marketing, which ultimately resulted in a boost in sales. If you can authentically be yourself in your business dealings and be a little vulnerable sometimes, you will be amazed by how many more people will connect with you. There are "perfect" pictures all over the place, and social media is filled with beautiful people doing fun things with lives that seem void of any conflict. But the reality is, the "bad" stuff usually isn't shared. So, if you put yourself out there and honestly let people know what you are feeling and thinking, I think you will be pleasantly surprised by the response you'll get more often than not. One of the most popular posts about the business that I ever had on Facebook was when I posted the pictures of our flooded-out space and talked about how overwhelming the whole thing was. Hundreds of people responded because I shared how I was genuinely feeling; I was vulnerable, terrified, sad, mad, frustrated, but also hopeful that brighter days were ahead. When we re-opened the studio after everything was repaired, so many people came in and were thrilled that we were back on our feet. People like to feel involved and included—people love a sense of community. The whole is greater than the sum of the parts, so leverage your community.

Nobody is going to give you permission to be more of yourself. Nobody will give you the green light to start accomplishing your dreams. Nobody is coming to help you with the work that you have to do in your business and on yourself. You will never feel ready enough or have enough money set aside or be at the perfect spot in your life to do the next thing. You just have to do it. YOU have to do the work, put the time in, make the sacrifices, put yourself and your business out into the world, and make your dreams a reality. Don't worry about what other people think or how people will perceive you. Just get out there and work on doing whatever it is that you want to do and give it 100 percent of yourself. Be authentic, be uniquely you, and don't take yourself too seriously—have fun!

Key Takeaways

- Don't worry about trying to always appear "perfect." Just be you.
- Show up for your team and customers every day.
- Stay humble and have fun.

Master Your Equipment

One of the ways that I made the day-to-day work of running the studio better for myself was figuring out how to use all the tools and equipment at my disposal. I became a master at using and managing the hardware and the software, the staff scheduling tools, managing our online customer-facing website, our point of sale tools, and the various social media platforms we routinely used. If I didn't know how to use or perform a task, I would look it up and learn. YouTube is an amazing resource! Check out your local community college, the Chamber of Commerce, or the local SBA office. All of them often have great classes that will help you learn a lot of the basic skills necessary to successfully run a business and master the tools many business use daily.

As you become more settled in your business, make the effort to learn how to use all the tools and equipment in your arsenal. Get comfortable learning the shortcuts and, when you have a few minutes, watch videos on how to expand your capabilities. This will save you time down the road as you learn how to speed up your daily tasks and reduce the amount of time you spend trying to figure out how to do things on the fly or when you are busy. Make a commitment to learn something new about your business line every day!

Once you learn how to use all of your equipment as efficiently as possible, you must share the knowledge with your team (if they will also be using the equipment). Create guides, hold training sessions, answer questions, and do whatever you can to make sure your team also knows how to use all the equipment for your business. Give them the tools to be able to operate efficiently even when you're not there to assist. Be receptive to feedback and recommendations for improvement. You should always actively work to remove roadblocks your team is experiencing.

One caveat to share with you: your time is not free. Your time is valuable, so if there are things you need to do that you don't know how to do, or don't want to do, then figure out how to find someone else to do it. Optimize your time. Focus on your long-term goals and invest your time in trying to accomplish them, not wasting time doing things that you can hire someone else to do for you, if they can do them better and more efficiently. There is a fine line here in learning how to perform simple tasks and mastering how to use your equipment in order to preserve the cost of labor, but if it takes way too much time to master something, then consider potentially hiring someone else to perform it for you. For instance, if you don't know how to fully use a social media platform like Instagram or Snapchat, reach out to your local community college and see if you can create an intern program to bring a marketing student on your team to help you out. Once you figure out what the most important tools are for your business (which ones can increase your sales and customer satisfaction), focus on mastering those tools or equipment.

Key Takeaways

- You must know how to use all of your equipment and be proficient with it— optimize its utility.
- Create guides to teach others how to use it.
- If it's too difficult or beyond your ability to figure out, then get help or hire someone else to do it.

Learn When to Say "No"

Learning to create boundaries in your business is oftentimes hard to do. You will find much more peace and tranquility day-to-day in your business life if you learn how to say "no."

"Thank you for the inquiry, but no, I cannot offer this free service."

"Thank you for the offer, but no, I won't be able to volunteer my time."

"Thank you for thinking of me, but as a general rule, I only donate to my personally selected charities, so no, I will not donate my resources."

It's okay to say "no." If you find yourself repeatedly in situations that make you uncomfortable saying "no," then create some personal rules so it's easier to refer to them if you need to. For instance, in the studio almost from the very first day we opened the doors, we were bombarded by requests for donations, coupons, discounts, and free products. Schools, youth groups, churches, non-profits—you name it and they would ask for a donation of some sort. In the beginning I said, "yes" to just about everything but it started to take over my life and became very expensive when all I was doing was spending all my time trying to create donations or prepare gift cards, so I put my foot down.

I created an email template that I would use to respond to every donation request I received. Basically, I indicated that, while we appreciated their endeavor, as a rule we only host one fundraising event in the studio per month for past customers. It was a very polite and friendly email that usually was successful in curtailing the never-ending requests we received for donation items. It also helped us to minimize the number of fundraising activities we hosted in the studio monthly. It's nice to be philanthropic when you can be, but choose carefully what you would like to do and don't forget that you have to turn a profit to stay in business. Keep a record of your charitable donations so you can write them off your taxes. Yes, sometimes the gifts and donations can lead to future sales, but be careful not to let it get out of hand.

My advice is to create your own rules and learn how to say "no" to things you really don't want to do or cannot do. Don't overextend yourself or make yourself crazy trying to do everything for everyone. Protect your peace and just say "no."

"No, I cannot offer this service for a reduced rate."

"No, I cannot provide a free gift for this fund-raising event."

"No, I don't have any coupons currently available."

"No, I cannot be in charge of this year's fundraising event. Thank you for thinking of me."

Key Takeaways

- It's okay to say "no."
- You don't always have to give a reason for saying "no."
- Accept that there will sometimes be consequences to saying "no."

Know the Value of Your Service

After the pandemic, all of our critical supplies (raw materials) became not just more expensive, but also harder to acquire. Nearly every supply we used for our studio became more scarce and jumped significantly in price—things that used to cost five cents per set quickly jumped to seventy-five cents per set. When we factored all of these price increases into the business model and what the cost of goods now was, it was significantly higher.

One of the flaws in our franchise business model is that every studio across the country had to charge the same rates for services, despite the fact that the expenses each studio incurred to run those services varied wildly across the nation. For instance, a lease in a small town in South Dakota might be ten dollars per square foot per month while a lease in California might be seventy-five dollars per square foot per month. The same goes for labor rates. The minimum wage today in Oklahoma is $7.25 per hour while, in New York, it is $13.20 per hour. The business required us to serve beer or wine.

In Virginia, the liquor licensing laws require you to include the cost of a glass of wine or beer into the cost of the event, while in New Jersey, the state liquor laws allow studios to offer Bring Your Own Beverage (BYOB) to their customers. Again, the cost to accomplish the task of offering an alcoholic beverage varies tremendously across the country. In some states, not only does a studio owner have to earn thousands of dollars annually to maintain a liquor license, but they also have to adhere to very strict rules (nobody under a certain age can be in the studio while alcohol is being served, for instance). I bring this up because you really need to hone in on the details of a business model and run some scenarios to estimate what your monthly gross and net profits may look like in your exact location. Talk to other small business owners in your zip code and try to uncover what other hidden costs there may be (annual business property tax, for instance).

I was the first studio in the country to raise my rates following the pandemic. I quickly realized that we would be operating at a loss if we didn't pass along the additional cost of goods to our customers. I worked with the other local studios to collectively petition the corporate office to raise our service rates. At first there was push back, but once we put together a formal proposal and sent it to the corporate office, it was approved. In hindsight, we probably didn't raise them enough (we just increased them by a few dollars), but it did help offset the new cost of goods slightly. When you see a shift in the business and can make small adjustments to remain profitable, take the action to do so. Perform some analysis and maybe hold some focus groups with customers to determine what kind of changes you can make that won't cause a negative impact to your business in the long run.

Don't be afraid to put yourself out there and ask the question, work on trying to fix the problem, adjust when the market changes, and know the nitty gritty financial details day-to-day so you recognize when there is a problem. Manage your inventory closely and track your labor costs so you can make the necessary adjustments when you need to. Don't bury your head in the sand and think that someone else will figure it out—they won't. If you own the business or if you are managing a department, then take the lead in making sure you are operating as efficiently as possible.

Key Takeaways

- Understand your industry and the value of your service.
- Don't be afraid to ask the difficult questions.
- Bring potential solutions to the table—be creative.

What's Your Exit Strategy?

Before you take off on an airplane ride as a passenger, you will be briefed by flight attendants about how to exit the plane in an emergency. Same thing when you are in a movie theater—you are given instructions for how to evacuate if necessary. Launching a business is no different: you should go into it realizing that, at some point, you'll want to get out of it. When we realized that we would not be extending our leases and that we weren't interested in signing another five-year franchise agreement, we realized we really needed to wrap our brains around how to get out of the business. We knew that we didn't want to close the businesses (they were all still successful and offering unique services to the community and we didn't want to dismantle the beautiful studios we built) so, having no idea how long it would take to find potential buyers, we began looking for a commercial realtor to help us through the process. Once we found a good broker and listed the first two locations, they sold pretty quickly and we were very pleased with the process. The last studio (the largest one), however, took much longer to sell and was quite a challenge.

What helped in this process was that we had hired a good accountant right from the beginning and so our business valuation and "books" or P/L (Profit and Loss) statements did not require much effort to put together and share with potential buyers that signed non-compete and confidentiality agreements. Take the time to be as organized as possible right from the very beginning, and then doing things like your taxes or other business transactions will be much easier. I used a very capable HR system to manage our team, and I'm so glad I did because it made capturing our labor metrics much easier to share with potential buyers. Sometimes it's just better to invest in professional services to make your life easier (if these are not skills or tools you easily possess).

Keep your business financial affairs in order, know the details, and always keep your mind open to different opportunities. And just as important as having a solid business plan to be profitable when starting out is having an exit strategy. When this new business or job is no longer fun or no longer profitable, how will you get out of it? If something happens to you, will someone be able to continue it? Go into it with your eyes open, recognizing that everything in life has cycles or phases. Be cognizant that, at some point, you'll be ready to move on and you'll need to position yourself and the business for that moment. Will you want to take the business public? Will you position yourself so that another company or person will buy you out? Visualize the beginning and the end of your time in the business. If you acknowledge and accept that, at some point, you will want to retire or transition away from the business, then it might not make sense to attach your name to it. Maybe "Celeste's Cupcakes" should be "Coastal Treats" instead—my point is to look at the opportunity from cradle to grave. Be realistic with yourself and structure the business endeavor in a logical manner that will survive the test of time.

Key Takeaways

- Accept that, at some point, you will want to leave the business.
- Think about the different options available to you to successfully depart the business.
- Help in the transition process as much as possible.

Keep Your Business and Personal Accounts Separate

Right from the very beginning, no matter how tempting it may be, keep your personal and business accounts 100 percent separate. Open a separate Amazon.com account if you need to, create a discrete Facebook account if you can, put your business resources in their own banking accounts—do whatever you can to draw an imaginary line in the sand between your personal and professional assets and accounts.

Keep in mind that long after you leave the business, you may still have refunds or other loose ends that you'll need to resolve. For instance, twelve months after the business was sold, I received a tax refund check from the IRS that I could only cash using the business checking account. I recommend that you hang on to the business banking accounts at least for eighteen to twenty-four months after you close or transfer the business. Same recommendation on your state filing status—you never know if you may be called to exercise it, so it's best to hang on to it at least for a little while. Our lease transfer agreement required that we be preserved as back-up guarantors on the lease and so, when the new owner wanted to negotiate some changes, it required that we sign them, and in order to do that, our current state filing as an LLC had to be current. Since I had closed the account, I had to pay a fee to have it reinstated; had I known this from the beginning, I would not have closed it so quickly.

I also had to keep access to the banking system where we had applied for the COVID inspired PPP—even though I had not used the account for some time, I still logged on periodically just to make sure I could access the account, and once the forgiveness application was activated, I would be able to apply for loan forgiveness. I was able to do this successfully for both round one and round two—amen!

Another area where I learned a tough lesson was in using the business email to create different accounts that I used in my business and in my personal life. As tempting as it may be (because sometimes it's just easier), I recommend that you keep all your business purchases completely separate from your personal purchases. If you are buying supplies for the business on Amazon, make sure you are using the business credit card and possibly a separate Amazon account. In my case, I had bought some rugs from a home furnishing store for the business, but commingled the business email and my personal phone number on the account. I didn't realize this until seven months after selling the business and making a personal purchase with the home furnishing store and having the new studio owner email me an itemized list of my purchase since they received the email. When I went in to change the email address, of course, I forgot the password and it was a lot of extra effort to get it fixed. Bottom line is to keep your business and personal accounts 100 percent separate with different phone numbers and different email/mail addresses.

Keep your tax and accounting records and be organized with all your financial documentation—you never know when you may need it for something. Also, keep in mind that there will be formal steps to take with your city, county, and state agencies to close out your corporation or transfer it to a new owner depending on the direction you are going. Basically, you will need to reverse the steps you took to create the business when you step away from the business or turn it over to someone else. Be mindful that this often takes a while and each agency requires their own discrete paperwork and processes. Keep accurate records of all your business filings.

Key Takeaways

- Do not commingle your personal and business/professional accounts or services.
- Keep accurate/factual records.
- Follow the correct process when opening and when closing your business.

Conclusion

I hope there was some piece of information in this little book that will be useful to you as you start off on your own business journey. It is impossible to cover every single issue or situation that may arise that you'll have to deal with. Just go into the endeavor knowing every day will bring a new trial or tribulation that you will have to overcome. There will always be a problem you have to figure out how to fix and a person that needs some of your undivided attention. Be ready for it and just make it your goal to give the best of yourself to each task. Follow the golden rule: "Do unto others as you would have them do unto you."

The business will also have financial ups and downs, so build some savings into your financial plan and prepare for challenging moments. Appreciate all that you learn along the way; it will help shape and develop you in profound ways that you cannot even fathom. One of the side effects of owning our small business was the impact it had on our teenaged kids. They both saw how hard we worked to be successful, and today each of them understands customer service intimately as well as small business accounting (better than many MBA students)! They know how important it is to keep a tidy, clean, and organized space that's welcoming for customers and staff. They know how critical it is to have open communication with your team and to have business tools to help manage the day-to-day business operations successfully and transparently. We've also made some extraordinary family friends along the way, which has truly turned out to be a huge blessing for us.

As you begin exploring the opportunity to start a small business, please do take the time to do a lot of research and be methodical about weighing all your options. Define for yourself what business success will look like and recognize that it will evolve over time.

Small businesses are the fabric of a community and so important to American society. We understand, appreciate and endeavor to frequent small businesses now more than ever before because we know intimately well how hard small businesses work to survive and to thrive. I wish you luck on your journey—may it be rewarding, enriching and wildly successful!

Appendix

Accion Opportunity Fund. https://aofund.org.

"Boots to Business." U.S. Small Business Administration (SBA). https://www.sba.gov/sba-learning-platform/boots-business. (The SBA connects entrepreneurs with lenders and funding to help them plan, start, and grow their business. Boots to Business, entrepreneurial education and training program for transition service members and their spouses.)

Colwell, Ken PhD MBA. *Starting a Business QuickStart Guide: The Simplified Beginner's Guide to Launching a Successful Small Business, Turning Your Vision into Reality*. ClydeBank Media LLC; 1st edition, 2019.

"D'Aniello Institute for Veterans & Military Families." Syracuse University. https://ivmf.syracuse.edu/.

"Find a Business For Sale." BizBuySell. https://bizbuysell.com.

"Find the Right Business or Franchise for You." BizQuest. https://www.bizquest.com.

"Franchise Opportunities." Franchise.com. https://www.franchise.com (Research opportunities for your area.)

International Franchise Association (IFA). https://www.franchise.org. (Franchise resources, small business news and advice. Invaluable resources to help you stay current with franchise and small business news and small business trends.)

"Office of Small Business Programs." Department of Defense. https://business.defense.gov.

Okoren, Nicolle. "How to Start a Small Business: Must-Have Checklist to Spark Success." Business.org. October 28, 2022. https://www.business.org/business/startup/how-to-start-a-small-business-checklist/.

SCORE. https://www.score.org. (SCORE business mentors can help you start, grow, or transition your business.)

Shopify. https://www.shopify.com. (Details of a variety of business opportunities.)

Stowers, Joshua. "How to Start a Business: A Step-by-Step Guide." Business News Daily. November 16, 2022. https://www.businessnewsdaily.com/4686-how-to-start-a-business.html.

Strauss, Steven D. *The Small Business Bible*. John Wiley & Sons: 2004.

"Your Complete Guide to Buying a Franchise Opportunity." Franchising.com. https://www.franchising.com. (Here you will find many resources to help you succeed in franchising.)

About the Author

Raquel Gladieux writes from her Annapolis, Maryland home with her toy Goldendoodle, Penny, by her side. She is married to a sailor (Andy) and is the mother of two fun-loving young adults (Connor and Carly) to whom she doles out "Mom hugs" to regularly. She is a 1995 graduate of the United States Naval Academy, a retired naval officer, and seasoned franchise business owner. She enjoys exploring real estate along the Chesapeake Bay, and cooking and boating with family and friends. When she is not on the water, she is supporting Information Technology Services.

Photo Credit to Laura Hatcher Photography

Review Requested:

We'd like to know if you enjoyed the book.
Please consider leaving a review on the platform
from which you purchased the book.

www.ingramcontent.com/pod-product-compliance
Lightning Source LLC
Chambersburg PA
CBHW030711220526
45463CB00005B/2000